Skills in English

Writing

Course Book

Level 2

Terry Phillips

Garnet
EDUCATION

Published by
Garnet Publishing Ltd.
8 Southern Court
South Street
Reading RG1 4QS, UK

ISBN 1 85964 783 9

British Library Cataloguing-in-Publication Data
A catalogue record for this book is available from
the British Library.

Production
Project manager: Richard Peacock
Editorial team: Nicky Platt, Lucy Thompson, John Bates,
                    Katharine Mendelsohn
Art director: David Rose
Design: Mark Slader
Illustration: Janette Hill, Karen Rose
Photography: Corbis/Sygma (Fabian Cevallos/Konow
                    Rolf), Digital Vision, Flat Earth, Image
                    Source, Photodisc

Garnet Publishing wishes to thank the following for their
assistance in the development of this project:
Dr Abdullah Al Khanbashi, Abderrazak Ben Hamida,
Maxine Gillway, Karen Caldwell and the Level 2 team at
UGRU, UAE University

Every effort has been made to trace the copyright holders
and we apologize in advance for any unintentional
omissions. We will be happy to insert the appropriate
acknowledgements in any subsequent editions.

Printed and bound
in Lebanon by International Press

Skills in English
Writing Level 2

Contents

Book Map

Theme	Input text type	Output text type	Writing skills
1 Education, How Do You Revise?	Notes	Advisory text	• Revision
2 Daily Life, Parents and Teenagers	Magazine article	Advisory text	• Giving an opinion: sentence level • Stating reasons • Giving an opinion: text level
3 Work and Business, How to Spend $10,000	Report with findings and recommendations	Report with findings and recommendations	• Writing a research report: sections
4 Science and Nature, The 8th Wonder of the World?	Progress report	Progress report	• Writing a progress report: sections
5 The Physical World, The UK and the USA	Encyclopedia article	Factual article	• Comparing two things
6 Culture and Civilization, There Are Two Ceremonies	Encyclopedia article	Factual article	• Writing a topic sentence • Linking sentences
7 They Made Our World, Biro and Marconi	Encyclopedia article	Factual article	• Summarising with topic sentences
8 Art and Literature, *Othello*	Research notes	Research notes + text	• Writing a plot • Using pronouns
9 Sports and Leisure, The Greatest Athlete in the World	Magazine article	Factual article	• Comparing more than two things • Paraphrasing
10 Nutrition and Health, Fish Is Good for Your Brain	Magazine article	Factual article	• Revision

Introduction

THIS COURSE IS THE WRITING COMPONENT of Level 2 of the *Skills in English* series. The series takes students in four levels from Elementary to Advanced level in the four skills, Listening, Speaking, Reading and Writing.

In addition, there is a remedial/false beginner course, *Starting Skills in English*, for students who are not ready to begin Level 1.

The writing component at each level is designed to build skills that help students survive in an academic institution where written assignments are wholly or partly in English.

This component can be studied on its own or with one or more of the other components, e.g., Listening and Reading.

The course is organised into themes, e.g., *Science and Nature, Art and Literature*. The same theme is used across the four skills. If, therefore, you are studying two or more components, the vocabulary and structures that you learn or practise in one component will be useful in another component.

Within each theme there are four lessons:

Lesson 1: *Vocabulary*
In the first lesson, you revise words from the theme that you have probably learnt already. You also learn some new words that you need to understand the texts in the rest of the theme.

Lesson 2: *Writing*
In this lesson, you practise skills that you have learnt in previous themes.

Lesson 3: *Learning new skills*
In this lesson, you learn one or more new skills to help you with writing.

Lesson 4: *Applying new skills*
In the final lesson, you use your new skills with another writing task. In most cases, the tasks in Lessons 2 and 4 have a similar structure, so you can check that your skills have improved.

www.skillsinenglish.com

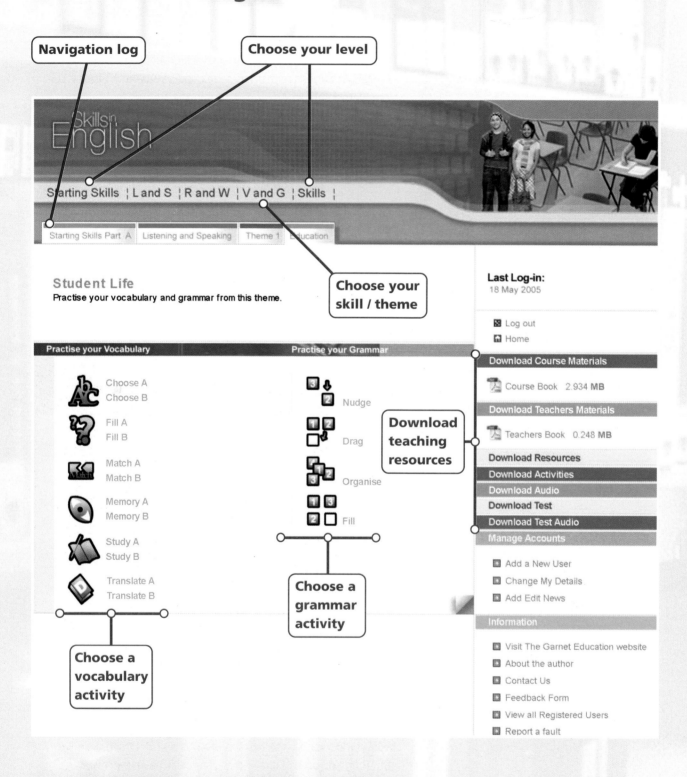

Navigation log

Choose your level

Starting Skills | L and S | R and W | V and G | Skills

Starting Skills Part A | Listening and Speaking | Theme 1 | Education

Choose your skill / theme

Student Life
Practise your vocabulary and grammar from this theme.

Last Log-in:
18 May 2005

Log out
Home

Practise your Vocabulary

Choose A
Choose B

Fill A
Fill B

Match A
Match B

Memory A
Memory B

Study A
Study B

Translate A
Translate B

Practise your Grammar

Nudge

Drag

Organise

Fill

Download teaching resources

Download Course Materials
Course Book 2.934 **MB**

Download Teachers Materials
Teachers Book 0.248 **MB**

Download Resources
Download Activities
Download Audio
Download Test
Download Test Audio
Manage Accounts

Add a New User
Change My Details
Add Edit News

Information

Visit The Garnet Education website
About the author
Contact Us
Feedback Form
View all Registered Users
Report a fault

Choose a grammar activity

Choose a vocabulary activity

Contact enquiries@garneteducation.com to obtain a password for access to full site information.

In this theme you are going to write some advice to students on learning and revising for a test.

Lesson 1: Vocabulary

You are going to learn some vocabulary you need to give advice on learning information and revising for a test.

Ⓐ Cover the red words. Complete the words below with a vowel letter (*a, e, i, o, u*) in each space. Then check your spelling with the red words.

1 ___ss___gnm___nt 5 f___rm
2 d___pl___m___ 6 ___nstr___ct___r
3 dr___ft 7 l___t___r___t___r___
4 f___c___lty

Ⓑ Which red word(s) has / have …
1 a doubled letter?
2 a silent letter?

Ⓒ Do the crossword. Choose a green word for each answer.

Across

1 …-choice questions have three or four answers, e.g., *Choose a, b, c or d.* (8)
6 The 'k' in *know* is a … letter. (6)
7 You should … before a test by looking carefully at all your notes. (6)
8 Try to … a new word to a word you already know, e.g., *choice* is the noun from the verb *choose*. (4)
9 An … question is a question with several possible answers. (4)

Down

2 You do a … test before the real test. (8)
3 Ask your teacher to tell you the … units for a test – in other words, the units you should study for the text. (8)
4 You must … your writing in a logical way. (8)
5 The letter 'o' is … in the word *book*. (7)

Ⓓ Look at the words in the table.
1 Complete the table.
2 Write a sentence with each noun and a sentence with each verb.

assignment (n)
diploma (n)
draft (n)
faculty (n)
form (n)
instructor (n)
literature (n)
doubled (adj)
link (v)
multiple (adj)
open (adj)
organise (v)
practice (n)
relevant (adj)
revise (v)
silent (adj)

verb	noun
	revision
test	
practise	
	organisation
draft	

Lesson 2: Writing

(A) Aisha is a student in the Education Faculty at Greenhill College. She is writing an assignment with the title 'How to learn'. Read her research notes. Match each red word from her notes to an explanation below.

1 doing different things with new information
2 doing something with new information
3 finding something strange about new information
4 hearing or reading new information lots of times
5 linking new information with old information

(B) Aisha must decide how to organise her text. She has written two drafts.

1 Read each draft. Complete the drafts with one word in each space.
2 How does each draft organise these parts?
   • ways of learning • explanations • examples?
3 Which organisation do you think is better? Why?

Learning

How to learn

There are five main ways of learning new information – and remembering it!

a Frequency (= often)

b Activity (= action)

c Variety (= different things)

d Association (= linking)

e Mnemonics (= helping the memory)

1 There are five main ways of learning new information.

The first way is frequency. The _____ way is activity. The _____ way is variety. The _____ way is association. The _____ way is mnemonics.

Frequency means hearing or reading new information lots of times. Activity _____ doing something with new information. Variety means _____ different things with new information. Association means linking new information with _____ information. Mnemonics means finding something strange about new _____.

For _____, you should write a new word ten times and say it to yourself. You _____ make up a sentence for a new word. You should try to use a _____ word three times in the next 24 hours. You should _____ a new word to a word you already know. _____ should find something strange about the _____ of a new word, e.g., doubled letters, or the _____, e.g., silent letters.

2 There are five main ways of learning new information.

The first way is _____. This means hearing or reading new information lots of times. For example, you should write a new word ten times and say it to yourself.

The second way is _____. This means doing something with new information. For example, you should make up a sentence for a new word.

The third way is _____. This means doing different things with new information. For example, you should try to use a new word three times in the next 24 hours.

The fourth way is _____. This means linking new information with old information. For example, you should link a new word to a word you already know.

The fifth way is _____. This means finding something strange about new information. For example, you should find something strange about the spelling of a new word, e.g., doubled letters, or the pronunciation, e.g., silent letters.

Lesson 3: Checking skills

Ⓐ You can make an English word by putting a vowel letter (*a, e, i, o, u*) in each space. What is the letter in each case?

1 ex___mple	**4** n___w	**7** s___mething	**10** w___rd
2 f___rst	**5** org___nise	**8** th___re	**11** m___ney
3 instruct___r	**6** sec___nd	**9** th___rd	**12** c___ntrol

Ⓑ You can make an English word by putting a pair of vowels in each space. What are the vowels in each case?

1 ab___ ___t	**4** h___ ___r	**7** m___ ___ns	**10** w___ ___k
2 expl___ ___n	**5** l___ ___rn	**8** sc___ ___nce	**11** rec___ ___ve
3 f___ ___rth	**6** m___ ___n	**9** sh___ ___ld	**12** fr___ ___nd

Ⓒ What is the missing silent letter in each word?

1 ans___er	**4** ___now	**7** math___matics	**10** ___rong
2 diction___ry	**5** lis___en	**8** av___rage	**11** b___ild
3 hist___ry	**6** lit___rature	**9** ___rite	**12** ta___k

Ⓓ All these words have doubled letters – vowels or consonants. Write the missing letters in the spaces.

1 a___ ___ress	**4** bi___ ___er	**7** ho___ ___er	**10** spe___ ___ing
2 agr___ ___	**5** di___ ___erent	**8** o___ ___osite	**11** o___ ___asion
3 be___ ___er	**6** f___ ___l	**9** sma___ ___	**12** a___ ___lication

Ⓔ Work in groups. Cover Draft 1 and Draft 2 (Lesson 2 Exercise B). How much can you remember?

1 What are the five main ways of learning new information?

2 Why is each way useful?

3 What example does Aisha give of each way when you are learning vocabulary?

Ⓕ Aisha made a table of information before she wrote her two drafts.

1 Look at Table 1. It shows the information she entered in the first row. Find this information in Draft 2.

2 Complete the other rows of the table. Take your information from Draft 2:

Table 1: How to learn new information		
Ways of learning	Why is each way useful?	Example action
Frequency	You learn information by hearing or reading it many times.	Write a new word 10 times and say it to yourself.
Activity	You learn information by _____ _____	Make up a sentence for _____ _____
Variety	You learn _____ _____	Try to use a new word three times _____
Association	You _____ _____	Link a new word to _____ _____
Mnemonics	_____ _____	Find something _____ _____

Lesson 4: Applying skills

Ⓐ Aisha must write another assignment with the title 'How to revise'. She has made a table of information (Table 1). Copy the table and ...
1 correct the grammar of the key questions. (Column 1)
2 correct the spelling of the possibilities. (Column 2)
3 complete the advice with the missing prepositions. (Column 3)

Table 1: How to revise		
Key questions	Possibilities	Advice
1. Which units of the course book you must revise for the test?	1. The hole book? Pats of the book?	1. Check your notes ____ all the relevant units. Copy missing notes _____ other students.
2. Which type of questions they will be in the test?	2. Esay topiks? Multipul choice qwestions? Questons with open ansers?	2. Ask your teacher _____ practice tests. Make practice tests _____ your friends.
3. When the test will be?	3. A long tim to rivise? A fue days?	3. Plan a study timetable ____ equal amounts _____ revision time _____ each day. Study _____ half an hour a day. Don't just study _____ 15 hours _____ the weekend.

Ⓑ What is the best way for Aisha to organize her text? Choose the best way.

> **a**
> Key question 1
> then possibilities 1
> then advice 1
> then key question 2, etc.

> **b**
> Key question 1
> then key question 2
> then key question 3
> then possibilities 1, etc.

Ⓒ When you write about the possibilities, use this pattern: *Perhaps ..., or perhaps ...*
Make sentences in pairs for the possibilities in the table.
  Example: *Perhaps the test will revise the whole book, or perhaps the test will only revise certain parts of it.*

Ⓓ When you write about the advice, use this pattern: *You should ... and you should ...*
Make sentences in pairs for the advice in the table.
  Example: *You should check your notes from the relevant units and you should copy missing notes from other students.*

Ⓔ Write your first draft. Begin:
There are three questions you must ask about the test.
Remember ...
1 to use pronouns – *Perhaps* **the test** *will revise the whole book, or perhaps* **it** ...
2 to cut repeated words after *and* – **You should** *check your notes from the relevant units and* ~~**you should**~~ *copy missing notes ...*

Ⓕ Exchange drafts with your partner and check each other's work. Then write a second draft for your teacher.

always *(adv)*

never *(adv)*

often *(adj)*

once *(adj)*

schedule *(n)*

social *(adj)*

sometimes *(adv)*

twice *(adv)*

usually *(adv)*

weekly *(adv)*

adult *(n)*

decision *(n)*

parent *(n)*

teenager *(n)*

In this theme you are going to write about relationships between parents and teenagers.

Lesson 1: Vocabulary

You are going to learn some of the vocabulary you will need to write about parents and teenagers.

A Cover the red words. Complete these words with one or more vowel letters in each space. Then check your spelling with the red words.

1 __lw__ys
2 n__v__r
3 __ft__n
4 __nc__
5 sch__d__l__

6 s__c__l
7 s__m__t __m__s
8 tw__c__
9 __s__ __lly
10 w__ __kly

B Discuss these questions. Use some of the red words.

1 What do you do with your mother and father in the evenings / at weekends / during the holidays?
2 Did you do different things when you were younger?

> I sometimes have a meal with my mother and father in the evening.

> When I was younger, I always had a meal with my mother and father in the evening.

C Study the graph.

1 Explain these words: *parent, teenager, adult*.
2 The line starts at 100 and goes to 0. What does this mean?
3 Give an example of a decision that a parent makes for a child.
4 Give an example of a decision that a teenager makes for himself / herself.
5 Draw another line on the graph to show who makes the decisions at different ages in your culture.

Figure 1: Who makes the decisions in British families?

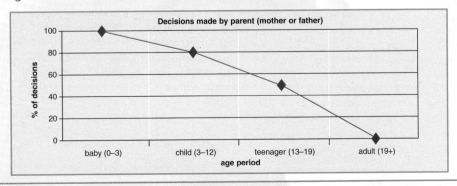

Lesson 2: Writing

(A) Adrienne Dumont is studying Sociology at Greenhill College.

1 Read the information opposite about Adrienne's course this semester.

2 Discuss the two main topics. Make two lists of advice:
 a for parents of teenagers
 b for teenagers

(B) Adrienne is researching the first topic. She is reading a magazine called *Good Parenting*.

1 Read the first three tips from the article. Notice how Adrienne has made notes.

2 Copy the table and make notes on the other tips.

	Advice	Example	Reason
1	teach her to admire good role models	religious leaders	bad role models = copy their behaviour?
2	encourage her to participate in society	local social clubs	the Devil finds work for idle hands
3	let her make her own decisions; involve her in family decisions	colour of her own bedroom / discussions about family holidays	may not rebel if part of the decision-making process

(C) Look at your notes. Add:

1 more **examples** for some of the tips.

2 more **reasons** for some of the tips.

3 one more **tip**, with examples and reasons – you need this for Lesson 3.

Good Parenting Magazine   Issue 323

Seven tips
for parents of teenagers

1 **Teach** your teenager to admire good role models, for example, religious leaders. If she admires bad role models, like rock stars, she may copy their behaviour.

2 **Encourage** your teenager to participate in society – local social clubs, for example. Remember that the Devil finds work for idle hands.

3 **Let** your teenager make her own decisions where possible. Involve her in family decisions. You could allow her to decide the colour of her own bedroom. You could discuss the family holidays with her. She may not rebel if she helped to make the decision.

4 **Remember** that most teenagers are idealistic. Many teenagers are vegetarians, for instance. Help them to channel the idealism. Don't make fun of it. Teenagers are seeing the world with new eyes. Perhaps their criticisms are correct.

5 **Admit** it when you are wrong – if you hit your teenager, for example, admit your mistake. Your teenager will be more likely to admit her own mistakes.

6 **Listen** to your teenager. Give her plenty of opportunities to talk about any problems, including at mealtimes. If you don't give her any attention, she may misbehave to get it.

7 **Follow** your own advice. Actions, they say, speak louder than words. You should not say drinking is bad and then drink yourself. Teenagers will not follow rules that you clearly break yourself.

Lesson 3: Learning new skills

Ⓐ Read these **reasons** for different pieces of **advice** to parents of teenagers. What must the advice be in each case?

1 If you don't give your teenager any attention, she may misbehave to get it. = *Listen to your teenager.*

2 Actions speak louder than words.

3 The Devil finds work for idle hands.

4 You cannot rebel if you are part of the decision-making process.

5 Perhaps their criticisms are correct.

Ⓑ Think of examples of each of the following:

1 good role models

2 bad role models

3 teenager's own decisions

4 family decisions

5 idealism in teenagers

6 wrong actions by parents

7 social activities

8 parents not following their own advice

Ⓒ Read Skills Check 1. Rewrite these sentences with introductions and *should*.

1 Teach your teenager to admire good role models.

2 Involve your teenager in family decisions.

3 Listen to your teenager.

4 Don't make fun of your teenager's idealism.

Ⓓ Read Skills Check 2. Write a good reason for advice 1, 2 and 3 in Exercise C. Use a conditional sentence.

Ⓔ Read Skills Check 3.

1 Find more examples of this pattern in the article in Lesson 2.

2 Write your extra tip from Lesson 2 Exercise C. Use the same pattern.

Skills Check 1

Giving an opinion (1)

We often use *should/n't* when we give opinions in English. But we can vary the sentence patterns with different introductory verbs and phrases.

Examples:

introduction	subject + verb	
I think that		
I believe that	*parents should*	*their own*
In my view,	*follow*	*advice.*
As I see it,		

Note:
Study these sentences. Notice the changes with *think* + negative.

don't ←		
I/think that	*parents shouldn't*	*fun of*
	make	*idealism.*

Skills Check 2

Stating reasons

We often use a conditional sentence to give the reason for an opinion.

Example:

If	present		*will / may*	
If	*they admire*	*bad role models,*	*they will they may*	*copy their behaviour.*

Skills Check 3

Giving an opinion (2)

When you give an opinion, it is a good idea to use this pattern:

Opinion then	*Parents should teach their teenagers to admire good role models,*
Example then	*for example, religious leaders or elder members of the family.*
Reason	*If they admire bad role models, they may copy their behaviour.*

Lesson 4: Applying new skills

Ⓐ You are going to write an essay entitled *Being a good teenager*. You may need some of these words. What are the missing vowels in each case?

1 adv____ce
2 beh____ve
3 behav____ ____ ____r
4 bel____ ____ve
5 decis____ ____n

6 ____b____y
7 opin____ ____n
8 r____sp____ct
9 sh____ ____ld
10 cr____t____c____se

Ⓑ Adrienne has written some sentences for the essay *Being a good teenager*. She has made grammar mistakes in each one. Correct the mistake in each sentence.

1 **a** I believe that teenagers respect their parents at all times.
  b For example, they should always to listen to their parents' ideas.
  c If they will not listen to them, they will not get the benefit of their experience.

2 **a** I believe that teenagers should not be rude to their parents.
  b He should not criticise them in public, for instance.
  c If they are rude, their parents stop helping them.

3 **a** To my opinion, teenagers should look after their parents in their old age.
  b They should invite their parent to live with them, for example.
  c If they don't look after their parents in old age, they do not repay the way their parents look after them in their childhood.

Ⓒ Complete the table for your essay. Try to think of at least five pieces of advice, with an example and a reason for each one.

	Advice	Example	Reason
1			
2			
3			
4			
5			

Ⓓ Write the first draft of your essay. Use the writing plan in Lesson 3, Skills Check 3, and some of the sentence patterns in Skills Checks 1 and 2 in the same lesson.

Ⓔ Exchange drafts with your partner. Tick (✔) good sentences. Mark with a question mark (?) any problems or mistakes.

Ⓕ Write the second draft. Give it to your teacher.

In this theme you are going to write a report.

Lesson 1: Vocabulary

You are going to learn some of the vocabulary you will need to write the report.

A Answer these questions about the red words.
1 What does an *applicant* do?
2 How can you *assist* someone?
3 What *benefits* can you get from a job, in addition to a *salary*?
4 What is the biggest source of *employment* in your town or area?
5 When can you do *overtime*?

B Students at Greenhill College have received the letter at the bottom of the page. Read the letter and say if these statements are true or false.
1 The letter is from Bill Beale.
2 The letter is about extra money from the college administrators.
3 The administrators want students to decide how to spend the money.
4 The college can spend the money on things like TVs, chairs and CD-ROMs.
5 Any student can write a letter to the administrators.
6 Students with ideas should write to Bill Beale.

C What are *equipment* and *study resources*? Make a list of items for each.

D What would you spend the money on? Choose the most important items from your lists in Exercise C.

Greenhill College

Dear Student

The Ministry of Higher Education has informed the administrators that they are providing Greenhill College with an extra $10,000 for the next academic year. They have advised us that they are not giving this money for salaries or to purchase furniture. It is to buy items to improve the equipment and study resources of the college.

In the past, the administrators decided how to spend any extra funds themselves. However, this year the authorities concluded that they should ask the students to assist in the decision-making process.

I am therefore requesting each tutor group to meet and discuss how to spend the additional money.

Please send a written report with recommendations to me by the 15th of this month.

Yours truly,

Bill Beale
on behalf of
The Administrators,
Greenhill College

applicant (n)

assist (v)

benefit (n)

employment (n)

overtime (n)

salary (n)

administrator (n)

conclude (v)

equipment (n)

furniture (n)

purchase (v)

recommendation (n)

report (n)

resource (n)

Lesson 2: Writing

(A) These words appear in the letter in Lesson 1.
Match words with a similar meaning.

1	extra	a	advised
2	informed	b	authorities
3	providing	c	concluded
4	money	d	funds
5	administrators	e	giving
6	buy	f	requesting
7	decided	g	purchase
8	asking	h	additional

(B) Imagine you are an administrator at Greenhill
College. You have just received the report on the
right.
1 How many sections are there in the report?
Make a list.
2 Cover the report. In which section will you
find the answer to each of the questions in
the box?
3 Uncover the report and check.

> a Who is the report from?
> b What is the report about?
> c How did the writers find out their
>   information?
> d What information did they find out?
> e What have they decided about the
>   information?
> f What do they recommend?

(C) Read the **Process** section carefully. Copy these
actions in order.

> appointed brainstormed checked chose
> reported back selected voted

(D) Read the other sections and write answers to the
questions.
Findings
1 Why did they reject some items?
2 How did they choose the final list?
Conclusions
Why did they choose the computers and
printers?
Recommendations
What do they recommend?

Introduction

This report is from a group of students in Semester 2.
We understand that the Ministry of Higher Education
is providing an extra $10,000. This money is for
equipment and study resources in the next
academic year. We are writing this report to make
recommendations for spending this money.

Process

We had our first meeting at the end of last month.
First, we brainstormed a number of different ways
to spend the money. Next, we selected the most
popular items and appointed two people, Ricardo
Moreno and Mona Saleh, to investigate the costs of
each item. They checked with the suppliers and
reported back at the beginning of the month. After
that, we voted on each item and chose the items to
recommend.

Findings

Table 1 shows the items and the approximate costs.
As you can see from the table, we found that two
of the items were too expensive. We rejected them
from consideration. For the other items, Table 2
shows the votes for each item.

Conclusions

In our opinion, the best improvements are Items 1 and
2 in Table 2 [bottom of page 17]. If there are extra
computers and printers in the Study Centre, more
students will be able to work there at the same time.

Recommendations

We think that the administrators should spend the
$10,000 on six computers and six printers for the
Study Centre.

Table 1: List of possible items

Item	**Cost** (approx.)
large-screen TV	$5,000*
interactive whiteboard	$3,000*
computer	$1,500
printer	$150
scanner	$300
web cam	$150
dictionary	$30
Wordbuilder CD-ROM	$50

* these items rejected = too expensive

Lesson 3: Learning new skills

A Reports with recommendations often contain five sections.

1 Cover the report in Lesson 2. Complete the names of the five sections in the box below.

2 Match the report sections and the information they contain.

3 Uncover the report and check the section names – including the spelling.

4 Read Skills Check 1 and check the section contents.

a Intro_____	**1**	your actions
b Pro_____	**2**	what the reader of the report should do now
c Find_____	**3**	your opinion
d Con_____	**4**	the writers + the purpose
e Rec_____	**5**	the facts

B You need different tenses and structures in most reports. Copy these sentences. Put the verb into the correct form in each case.

1 **a** We (understand) that the Ministry of Higher Education (provide) an extra $10,000.

 b We (write) this report (make) recommendations for (spend) the money.

2 **a** We (select) the most popular items.

 b We (vote) on each item.

3 **a** We (find) that two items (be) too expensive.

 b Table 2 (show) the votes for each item.

4 **a** In our opinion, the best improvements (be) Items 1 and 2 in Table 2.

 b If there (be) extra computers and printers in the Study Centre, more students (be able) (work) there at the same time.

5 We (think) that the administrator (spend) the $10,000 on six computers and six printers for the Study Centre.

C Read Skills Check 2. Check your answers.

Table 2: Items + votes

Item	Votes
computer	10
printer	8
Wordbuilder CD-ROM	7
scanner	6
dictionary	5
web cam	3

Skills Check 1

Writing a report with recommendations (1)

Reports often contain five sections. Each section contains answers to one or two questions from the reader:

1 Who is the report from? Why are you writing it?

2 How did you get the information in the report?

3 What information did you find out?

4 What did you decide about the information?

5 What should I do now?

Skills Check 2

Writing a report with recommendations (2)

Most reports have sections about the past, the present and the future. Therefore, you need to use different tenses and structures in each section:

1 We **understand** that …
 We **are writing** this report to …

2 We **had** meetings …
 We **considered** …
 We **made** a list …

3 We **found** that …
 We **discovered** that …

4 We **concluded** that the best way to spend the money was …
 If we **do** X, Y **will happen**.

5 We **think** that you **should** …
 We **recommend** …

Lesson 4: Applying new skills

A Complete the table with the missing words.

	verb	noun
1		conclusion
2	decide	
3		findings
4	improve	
5	recommend	
6		introduction
7		discussion
8	report	

B Rewrite each word with the correct spelling.

1	undrestand	
2	provideing	
3	eqipment	
4	resorces	
5	branestormed	
6	selekted	
7	investigat	
8	opinon	
9	administraters	
10	computors	

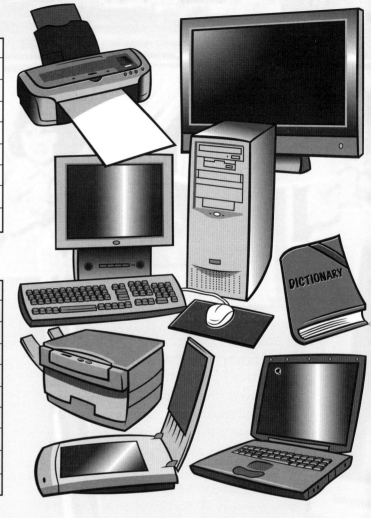

C Imagine that you have received the same sort of letter as the students at Greenhill College (Lesson 1). Work in groups, but make your own notes during all the discussions.
1 Brainstorm different ways to spend the money. Make a list.
2 Select the most popular items.
3 Find out the cost of each item – use the Internet or, if you can't find the real costs, guess.
4 Reject items that you think are too expensive.
5 Vote on the rest of the items. Make sure you have good reasons for voting for an item. Make sentences with *If … .*

D Work on your own.
1 Make a table of the most popular items with the approximate cost (Table 1). Note any items rejected because of cost.
2 Make another table of the votes for the selected items (Table 2).
3 Write the first draft of your report in five sections.

E Work in your groups again. Read all the other reports from the people in your group. Make notes of any improvements you can make to your report.

F Write a second draft of your report and give it to the teacher.

In this theme you are going to write a progress report.

Lesson 1 Vocabulary

You are going to learn some vocabulary that you need to write the progress report.

A Look at the graph of a project.

1 What is the name of the project?
2 What is the unit of measurement?
3 How many phases are there?
4 When did Phase 2 start?
5 What was the total of all three phases in 2002?
6 When was there a big increase in the total?
7 When was there a steady increase in Phase 3?
8 When was there a decrease in any of the phases?

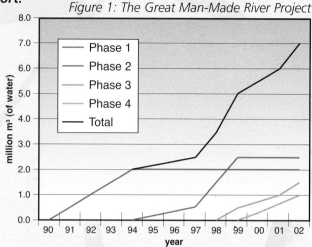

Figure 1: The Great Man-Made River Project

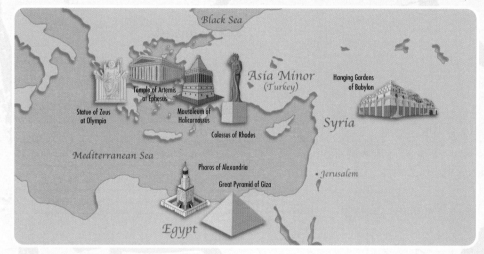

B Read the text. Look at the illustration.

The Ancient Greeks made a list of the Seven Wonders of the World. They chose structures that were difficult to build. Only one exists today – the pyramids at Giza, near Cairo in Egypt.

Now, the government of Libya claims it is building the Eighth Wonder. It is the Great Man-Made River Project in the Sahara desert. The project aims to bring fresh water from the desert to the coast. It involves laying 3,500 kilometres of water pipes. The project has several phases, but the latest progress report shows that it is achieving its aim.

At present, seven million cubic metres of fresh water are flowing every day. That's enough drinking water for all the people of Libya, with plenty left for agriculture.

C Read the facts and figures. Do you think the Great Man-Made River is a wonder of the world?

D What are the wonders of your country – ancient and modern?

> **Facts and figures**
> The project used:
> **cement** – you could build a road from Abu Dhabi to London with the cement.
> **lorries** – they travelled the distance to the sun and back.
> **steel wire** – it could go round the Earth 280 times.
> **stones** – you could build 20 Great Pyramids with the stones.

average *(adj)*

decrease *(n)*

graph *(n)*

increase *(n)*

steady *(adj)*

unit of measurement *(n)*

achieve *(v)*

aim *(n)*

construct *(v)*

facts and figures *(n)*

fresh (water) *(adj)*

project *(n)*

structure *(n)*

Lesson 2: Writing

You are going to read a progress report on the Great Man-Made River Project.

A Look at the map of the project. Can you see how it is divided into phases?

B Progress reports usually have sections with headings.
  1 Number the headings under the map in a logical order.
  2 Scan the sections of the report opposite. Check your answers.
  3 Write each section heading in the correct space.

C Read the progress report.
  1 Make notes on the form under the report. Only put the facts and figures.
  2 Check your notes in pairs.

D Ask and answer in pairs.

Lesson 3: Learning new skills

A Play noughts and crosses. Make a good question about a project with each word from the grid.

B There are grammar mistakes in the sentences below from a progress report.
  1 Read each sentence. Can you see what's wrong?
  2 Read the Skills Check.
  3 Rewrite each sentence correctly.

a Introduction	*The exact cost of the project not clear.*
b Introduction	*The government pays for the project.*
c Background	*In 2002, the government asks if the project is possible.*
d Progress to date	*Last year, the company finish Phase 1.*
e In the future	*Phase 4 will starting next year.*
f Final achievements	*The project makes the roundabouts more beautiful.*

C Cover the report. Look at the notes you made in Lesson 2. Write one full sentence to answer each question.
  Example:
  1 Where is the project? *Libya*
  You write: *The project is in Libya.*

Background	☐

Final achievements	☐

In the future	☐

Introduction	☐

Progress to date	☐

future	cost	background
name	construction	pay
aim	achieve	progress

D Several sentences in *Background* have the same basic structure. How does the writer vary the structure?

E What words or expressions does the writer use in *Progress to date* to show the order of events?

This is a progress report on a major engineering project in Libya called the Great Man-Made River Project (GMR). A South Korean company called Dong Ah is doing the majority of the construction work. Local construction companies are assisting Dong Ah. The first half of the project cost $10.2 billion. The exact cost of the second half is not clear at present, but it will be approximately $10 billion. The Libyan government is paying for the project. The aim of the project is to bring fresh water from the desert to the coast.

In 1960, oil companies looking for oil in the Sahara found a huge reservoir of water deep under the desert. The Libyan government asked scientists in 1974 if the project was possible. Ten years later, they decided to go ahead with the project. They divided it into five phases. Construction of GMR started in 1990.

Firstly, in Phase 1, pipes brought two million cubic metres of water to Benghazi. Next, pipes brought 2.5 million cubic metres of water to Tripoli in Phase 2. After that, pipes brought an extra 1.5 million cubic metres to Benghazi in Phase 3.

Phase 4 will bring one million cubic metres to Tobruk. Finally, Phase 5 will connect the pipes in Phase 1 and Phase 2. It will start soon, and it will probably end in 2006 or 2007.

Firstly, the project will bring fresh water to the whole population of Libya. Secondly, GMR will produce an extra 1,500 square kilometres of agricultural land.

1 Where is the project?	Libya
2 What is the name of the project?	
3 Who is doing the construction work?	
4 What is the cost of the project?	
5 Who is paying for the project?	
6 What is the aim of the project?	
7 What is the background to the project?	
8 What is the progress to date?	
9 What will happen in the future?	
10 What will the project achieve?	

Lesson 4: Applying new skills

A Match the words to make phrases from the text in Lessons 2 and 3.

1 progress	**a** $10 billion
2 engineering	**b** ahead
3 Libyan	**c** companies
4 oil	**d** cost
5 exact	**e** government
6 approximately	**f** land
7 present	**g** metres
8 fresh	**h** phases
9 go	**i** project
10 five	**j** report
11 cubic	**k** time
12 agricultural	**l** water

B Complete these paragraph headings from a progress report.

1 Intro_____

2 Back_____

3 Pro_____

4 In the _____

5 Final _____

C We have seen that, in a way, a report answers questions from the reader.

What questions does each paragraph in Exercise B answer? Remember – the *Introduction* answers lots of questions.

D You are going to write a progress report on an engineering project that is happening now in your country.

If possible, it should be a project that will improve the environment.

1 Do some research and make notes on the form below.

2 Write the first draft of your progress report.

3 Exchange drafts with a partner. Tick (✓) good sentences. Mark with a question mark (?) any problems or mistakes.

4 Write a second draft of your progress report. Show it to your teacher / instructor.

Where is the project?	
What is the name of the project?	
Who is doing the construction work?	
What is the cost of the project?	
Who is paying for the project?	
What is the aim of the project?	
What is the background to the project?	
What is the progress to date?	
What will happen in the future?	
What will the project achieve?	

In this theme you are going to write a text comparing your country with another country in the same region.

Lesson 1: Vocabulary

You are going to learn some vocabulary you need to compare countries.

Ⓐ Where is your country? How could someone find it easily on a world map? Use some of the red words.

Ⓑ Describe one of the other countries on the map above. Can your partner work out which country you are describing?

Ⓒ Complete the crossword with a green word in each space. Find the hidden word.

1 normal weather	
2 edge of a country	
3 most important	
4 the number of people	
5 place	
6 size of a country	
7 Africa, Asia, etc.	
8 oil production, steel-making	
9 farming	

Ⓓ How much do you know about your country? Talk about your country, using the green words.

Example:

My country has a border with Saudi Arabia.

continent *(n)*

fertile *(adj)*

region *(n)*

the Equator *(n)*

agriculture *(n)*

area *(n)*

border *(n)*

climate *(n)*

continent *(n)*

industry *(n)*

location *(n)*

main *(adj)*

population *(n)*

Lesson 2: Writing

Ⓐ You are going to read a text about two countries. It compares the countries, using facts from the table below.
Complete the text with the correct fact in each space.

Ⓑ Work in pairs. Cover the text and look at part of the table.
Student A: Look at the information about the UK.
Student B: Look at the information about the USA.
1 Write five sentences from the information. Make mistakes of fact in two of your sentences.
   Examples:
   The UK is located in Western Europe. **(True)**
   The area of the UK is just over 345,000 square kilometres.
   (False – it's just under 245,000.)
2 Show your sentences to your partner. Can he / she identify the false sentences and correct them?

Ⓒ Look at the text again. Find and underline the words in the yellow box.

Ⓓ Cover the text. Write five sentences comparing the two countries.
Use words from the box.
Example: *The USA is bigger than the UK in area.*

> bigger hotter colder
> both whereas while

The two main countries in the English-speaking world are the United Kingdom and the United States of America. The UK is located in _____, whereas the USA is part of the _____ continent. The UK has one short land border, with _____, while the USA has two very long land borders – one in the _____ with Canada and one in the _____ with Mexico.

In both the UK and the USA, of course, English is the main language. However, in the USA a large number of people speak _____.

The USA is much larger than the UK, at just under _____ million square kilometres, whereas the UK is just over _____ thousand square kilometres. The USA is also much bigger in population. There are just over _____ million people in the USA, compared with just under _____ million in the UK.

The capital of the USA, Washington, DC, is hotter in summer than London. The temperature is _____°C compared with 22°C. However, it is colder in winter: -3°C compared with _____°C.

Both countries have a lot of agricultural land – _____% in the UK against _____% in the USA, but in neither country is agriculture the main industry. In the UK, the main industries are services – retailing and _____, whereas in the USA the main industries are oil and _____.

Country	UK	USA
Region	Western Europe	North America
Borders	The Republic of Ireland	Canada (north), Mexico (south)
Area	244,800 km²	9.6 m km²
Population (million)	59.8	281
Language(s)	English	English (Spanish = large number)
Climate	London summer: 22°C; winter: 2°C	Washington, DC, summer: 31°C; winter: -3°C
Agricultural land	71%	45%
Industry	services = retailing, banking	oil, steel

Lesson 3: Learning new skills

A Cover the opposite page. Write the missing vowels in these words used in writing comparisons.

1 b__th
2 m__ch
3 wh__l__
4 wh__r__s
5 h__w__v__r
6 c__mp__r__

B How can you compare two things in English? There is a mistake in each of these sentences. Can you find it and correct it?

1 In both the UK also the USA, English is the main language.
2 Both of countries have a lot of agricultural land.
3 The USA is more larger then the UK.
4 The temperature is 22°C compared 31°C.
5 The UK has 60 million people where the USA has 280 million.

C Read Skills Check 1 and check your answers to Exercise B above.

D You can also compare two things with comparative adjectives.

1 Correct the spelling of the adjectives in the yellow box.
2 Can you remember or work out the spelling rules?
3 Read Skills Check 2 and check.

| hoter | coldder | largeer | warmmer |
| smaler | biger | cooler | weter | dryer |

Comparing two things (1)

There are special words in English when two things are **the same**, e.g., *both*.

Both	X	and	Y	are / have ...
Both	countries			are / have ...
Both	of them			are / have ...

When two things are **different**, use **whereas** or **while**. This tells the reader the next piece of information is about the other thing.

Examples:

*The UK is located in Western Europe, **whereas** the USA is part of the North American continent.*
*The UK has one short land border, **while** the USA has two long land borders.*

Comparing two things (2)

We use **comparative adjectives** to compare two things.

Examples:

*Washington is **hotter** in summer **than** London.*
*It is **colder** in winter.*

We make the comparative with adj + *er*, but if the adjective ends in:

1 *e* = add *r*, e.g., *larger*
2 CVC = double C, e.g., *hotter*
3 *y* – change to *i*, e.g., *drier*

Lesson 4: Applying new skills

A Complete these sentences with a comparative adjective in each space.
Be careful with the spelling.

1 The USA is much _____ than the UK. It is 9.6 million square
kilometres compared with just under 245,000.

2 The UK has a _____ population than the USA. It has 60 million
people compared with 281 million.

3 London is _____ in summer than Washington, DC. The temperature is 22°C compared with 31°C.

4 London is _____ than Washington in the winter. The temperature is 2°C compared with -3°C.

B You are going to compare your country with another country in the same region.

1 Choose a country from your region. Write the name of the country at the top of the second column of
the table below. Research the country to complete the rest of the column. Check your research
information with other people who chose the same country.

2 Write the name of your country at the top of the third column. Research information to complete the
rest of the column. Check your research information with other people from the same country.

Country			Para
Region			
Borders			
Area			
Population			
Language(s)			
Climate			
Agricultural land			
Industry			

C Look at the text in Lesson 2 again. How does the writer organise the information into paragraphs? Write the
correct paragraph number against each section of the table.

D Write the first draft of your text. Use structures and words from the Skills Checks in Lesson 3 and from the
sentences in Exercise A above.

E Exchange your draft with a person who has chosen the same country to compare with. Tick (✓) good
sentences. Mark with a question mark (?) any problems or mistakes.

F Write the second draft of your text. Show it to your instructor / teacher.

In this theme you are going to write about marriage in your country.

Lesson 1: Vocabulary

You are going to learn some of the vocabulary you will need for your essay.

A Discuss these questions. Use some of the red words.

1 What is the name of the biggest festival in your country?
2 When do you see balloons in the street in your country?
3 Is there a special festival to mark the harvest? What happens?
4 Do you like parades? What was the last one you saw?

B In Lesson 2 you are going to read a text about Islamic weddings in India. Here are some sentences from the text. Complete the sentences with the green words. Use the definitions to help you.

1 There are a number of _____ before the wedding.
2 At the _____ ceremony, a boy and a girl agree to get _____.
3 The parents of the couple decide on a date for the _____.
4 A henna artist puts henna on the hands and feet of the _____.
5 After the wedding, the _____ contract is presented.
6 The bride's father tells the _____ to take care of his daughter.

ceremony an event in a public place with a lot of special activities

married the adjective from *marry*

wedding the event at which a man and woman get married

bride a woman who is getting married

marriage the noun from *marry*

engagement the agreement to marry at a later date

groom a man who is getting married

C Study the green words. Which ones ...

1 have doubled letters?
2 end in *e*?
3 have two vowels together?
4 have the same vowel twice (but not together)?
5 have the same vowel three times (but not together)?
6 have the same consonant twice (but not together)?

D Test each other on the green words.

Student A
Give one of the definitions.

Student B
Identify the word and write it down.

balloon (n)	
festival (n)	
harvest (n)	
neighbour (n)	
parade (n)	
bride (n)	
ceremony(ies) (n)	
engagement (n)	
groom (n)	
marriage (n)	
married (adj)	
wedding (n)	

Lesson 2: Writing

You are going to read about Islamic weddings in India.

(A) Look quickly at the article opposite. Find and copy the events into the correct places in Table 1 opposite. Write any English translation in brackets after special words.

(B) Look again at the text. Compare Islamic weddings in India with traditional weddings in your country.
   1 Tick (✓) five things that are the same in your culture.
   2 Mark with a cross (✗) five things that are different.

(C) Write sentences comparing Indian culture with your culture.
   1 Write five sentences with *both*.
      Example: *In both cultures there is an engagement ceremony before the wedding ceremony.*
   2 Write five sentences with *whereas* and *while*.
      Example: *In Indian culture, the bride wears yellow, whereas in … culture she wears white.*

(D) Number your sentences in Exercise C in a logical order. Then rewrite the sentences as two paragraphs.

Lesson 3: Learning new skills

(A) Put these words into pairs. Explain your choices.

| boy bride couple father |
| girl groom man parent |
| *wali* woman both parties |
| man and woman |

(B) In Indian culture, who …
   1 becomes engaged?
   2 decides on a date for the wedding?
   3 arrives with his wedding procession?
   4 usually wears a long skirt and blouse?
   5 reads verses from the *Holy Qur'an*?
   6 agrees on the wedding gift?
   7 signs the marriage contract?
   8 sits together after the wedding dinner?
   9 gives the bride's hand to the groom?
   10 holds the *Holy Qur'an* above the bride's head?

(C) Every paragraph needs a topic sentence.
   1 Read Skills Check 1.
   2 Write a suitable topic sentence for each of the paragraphs you wrote in Lesson 2 Exercise D.

(D) You must link sentences in a paragraph.
   1 Read Skills Check 2.
   2 Read each paragraph about Indian weddings again. There is an extra sentence for each paragraph under the table. But where should it go? Write the number of the extra information in the best place in the paragraph.

Before the wedding
There are a number of ceremonies before the wedding. At the *mangni* (or engagement) ceremony, a boy and a girl agree to get married. (1) The girl wears a dress that she gets as a present from the boy's family. At the *mangni*, the parents of the couple decide on a date for the *nikaah*, or wedding.

The *mehndi* (henna) ceremony takes place at the bride's home on the evening before the wedding. During the ceremony, the women sing traditional songs.

During the wedding
There are several ceremonies on the day of the wedding. Weddings can take place at the bride's home, the groom's home, or at a local hall. The groom arrives at the location with his *baraat*, or wedding procession.

The groom drinks sherbet with the bride's brother. The bride usually wears a *sharara*, which is a long flowing skirt and blouse.

A *maulvi*, or priest, conducts the ceremony in front of close relatives of the bride and groom, including the *walis*, i.e., the fathers of the bride and the groom.

The *maulvi* reads selected verses from the *Holy Qur'an*. The *nikaah* ends with the *ijab* and *qubul* – in other words, the proposal and acceptance.

There is one other important matter to decide on the day of the *nikaah*. The older relatives of the man and woman agree on the *mehar*, or wedding gift, from the groom's family to the bride's family.

After the *nikaah*, the marriage contract, or *nikaahnama*, is presented. It contains the rules for both parties. It is signed by the groom, the bride, the *walis* and the *maulvi*.

The women and the men have dinner separately. After dinner, the couple sit together for the first time, on either side of the *Holy Qur'an*. This ceremony is called *aarsi mussahaf*. Their heads are covered by *dupattas* (traditional scarves). They read prayers under the direction of the *maulvi*.

After the wedding
There are two main ceremonies on the day after the wedding. The bride's father gives her hand to the groom. This ceremony is called the *rukhsat*, or farewell. The bride says goodbye and leaves to go to the groom's house. The groom's mother holds the *Holy Qur'an* above the head of the bride as she enters her new home for the first time after the wedding.

Table 1: Ceremonies in an Islamic wedding in India

Before the wedding	During the wedding	After the wedding
mangni (engagement)		

1 They exchange rings.
2 A henna artist puts the *mehndi* on the girl's hands and feet.
3 Musicians play traditional songs when the groom arrives.
4 The groom wears a *sherwani*, a traditional coat.
5 The *walis* play an important role in the ceremony.
6 Usually, the groom's side proposes and the bride's side accepts.
7 The groom's family can pay the *mehar* at the wedding or later.
8 The contract includes the right of the wife to divorce her husband.
9 The name comes from the word for mirrors (*aarsi*), because the couple can only see each other in mirrors.
10 He tells the groom to take care of her.

Lesson 4: Applying new skills

A Information appears in an English sentence in several common patterns.
Look at each set of four pieces of information.
  1 Number the sections of each set in the correct order to make a good sentence.
  2 Write out each sentence. Be careful with your punctuation.
  3 Look at all of your sentences. What is the common pattern?

a | traditional songs | during the ceremony | the women | sing

b | the groom | with the bride's brother | sherbet | drinks

c | from the *Holy Qur'an* | reads | the priest | selected verses

d | contains | the rules | for both parties | the contract

e | the bride's hand | gives | the bride's father | to the groom

B These sentences have the same basic pattern. But there is extra information – about the subject, the object or the time.
  1 Number the sections of each set in the correct order to make a good sentence.
  2 Write out each sentence. Be careful with your punctuation.

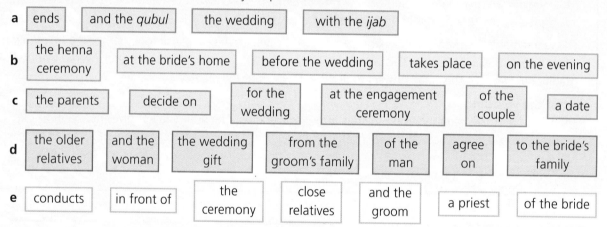

a | ends | and the *qubul* | the wedding | with the *ijab*

b | the henna ceremony | at the bride's home | before the wedding | takes place | on the evening

c | the parents | decide on | for the wedding | at the engagement ceremony | of the couple | a date

d | the older relatives | and the woman | the wedding gift | from the groom's family | of the man | agree on | to the bride's family

e | conducts | in front of | the ceremony | close relatives | and the groom | a priest | of the bride

C You are going to write about weddings in your culture.
  1 Copy and complete Table 1. Put English translations of any special words.
  2 Write three paragraphs, following the chronological order of information in the table. Use the basic sentence patterns from Exercises A and B above.
  3 Write a topic sentence for each paragraph.
  4 Exchange drafts with a partner. If you come from the same culture, decide if the factual content is correct. Otherwise, check the information with the table your partner has made. Tick (✓) any good points. Mark (?) any problems.
  5 Correct any mistakes of fact, spelling, punctuation and grammar, and make a second draft.
  6 Give your second draft to your teacher / instructor.

Table 1: Ceremonies in a wedding in my culture

Before the wedding	During the wedding	After the wedding

In this theme you are going to write about a famous invention in the field of communication.

Lesson 1 Vocabulary

You are going to learn some of the vocabulary you will need to write about the invention.

A Three of the red words are past simple verbs. What is the infinitive in each case? Write the word after each verb. Be careful with the spelling.

B Cover the red words. Correct the spelling.

1 controll _____ 4 infent _____

2 drov _____ 5 saled _____

3 flue _____

C Can you …

1 drive a jet?   3 sail in a submarine?   5 ride a horse?

2 join the navy?   4 row a plane?   6 control a car?

D In Lesson 2 you are going to read about a famous invention. Here is the outline of the text. Choose a green verb for each space. Make any necessary changes.

Ladislo Biro was born in Hungary in 1900. He had to use a pen in his job, but it _____ very well. He _____ to make a better pen. At first, there were problems with the new invention, but Biro _____ several solutions. He _____, for example, that he needed a new kind of ink. He _____ the problems and the pen worked. However, he _____ his invention in his own country. He moved to Argentina and began to _____ the pen there. He _____ his first pens to the British and American governments. Sales _____ 50,000 a week by 1945.

E In Lesson 4 you are going to write about another famous invention. You may need the nouns from some of the red and green verbs. Complete the table. Be careful with spelling.

1	decide	
2	develop	
3	invent	
4	produce	
5	sell	
6	solve	

control (v)

drove (v)

flew (v)

invent (v)

jet (n)

navy (n)

rode (v)

row (v)

sailed (v)

submarine (n)

decide (v)

develop (v)

produce (v)

reach (v)

realise (v)

sell (v)

solve (v)

think of (v)

work (v) (= do the job correctly)

Lesson 2: Writing

(A) Look at the topic sentences opposite. Answer the questions.
1 Who is the text about?
2 When was he born?
3 What nationality was he?
4 What did he invent?
5 When did he invent it?
6 Where did he develop his invention?

(B) Topic sentences do not answer all the reader's questions. Look at the underlined words / phrases. Think of questions to find out extra information in each case.
Example:
Biro had to use a <u>fountain pen</u> in his work as a <u>proof-reader</u>.
What's a fountain pen?   What does a proof-reader do?

BALLPOINT PEN

METAL BALL   INK   BARREL

(C) Uncover the other sentences. Find the sentences that continue each paragraph. Find answers to your questions in Exercise B.

FOUNTAIN PEN

CENTRAL FEED   END CAP

NIB   PLUNGER

BARREL

(D) Cover the topic sentences. Write a good topic sentence for each paragraph.

Lesson 3: Learning new skills

(A) Explain the meaning of these words. They are all connected with pens.

> ballpoint   cartridge   ink   fountain pen   nib   inkwell   smudge

(B) Complete this summary of the invention of the ballpoint pen. Use a preposition or an adverb in each space.

Ladislo Biro was born ____ 1900 ____ Hungary. Biro had ____ use a fountain pen ____ his work ____ a proof-reader. However, there were problems ____ the fountain pen ____ Ladislo's work. Ladislo decided to make a better pen. He thought ____ several solutions. Biro could not develop his invention ____ Hungary. ____ 1940, Ladislo and Georg moved ____ Argentina. The new pens were an immediate success.

(C) Look again at the text in Exercise B.
1 What is interesting about all of the sentences?
2 Read the Skills Check and check.

(D) The writer has done more research – see under the text opposite. Decide where to put each extra sentence.
Example:

Topic sentence	Ladislo Biro was born in 1900 in Hungary.
Paragraph	He had a number of jobs as a young man – journalist, painter, sculptor.
	He even worked as a hypnotist for a short time.
	He had a brother called Georg, who was a chemist.

Topic sentences		Other sentences in the paragraph
1 Ladislo Biro was born in 1900 in Hungary.	**a**	A proof-reader checks manuscripts from writers and makes corrections on them. Ladislo used a fountain pen in his work. Fountain pens use normal ink, but they carry the ink in a special cartridge. This means that you do not have to keep dipping the nib into an inkwell.
2 Biro had to use a <u>fountain pen</u> in his work as a <u>proof-reader</u>.	**b**	Finally, he decided to put a small ball in the tip of the pen instead of a nib. As the pen moved along the paper, the ball turned. It picked up ink from the ink cartridge and left it on the paper. By 1938, he had a ballpoint pen that worked.
3 However, there were <u>problems</u> with the fountain pen for Ladislo's work.	**c**	He had a number of jobs as a young man – journalist, painter, sculptor. He had a brother called Georg, who was a chemist.
4 Ladislo decided to make a <u>better</u> pen.	**d**	He knew that the ink used in newspaper printing dried quickly. He asked his brother to make a similar ink for a new kind of pen. However, the thicker ink would not flow through a normal nib. Ladislo realised that he needed to invent a new nib.
5 He thought of several <u>solutions</u>.	**e**	There, in 1943, Biro got money to develop his pen. He registered a patent in the same year.
6 Biro <u>could not develop his invention</u> in Hungary.	**f**	Sales reached 50,000 a week in 1945. By 1956, they were a quarter of a million a day. Now, more than 15 million biros are sold every day in 160 countries.
7 In 1940, Ladislo and Georg <u>moved</u> to Argentina.	**g**	The Second World War was coming, and the Biro brothers had to leave their home country.
8 The new pens were an <u>immediate</u> <u>success</u>.	**h**	Firstly, the ink took a long time to dry, so he had to be careful not to smudge his corrections. Secondly, the pen did not hold very much ink, so he had to keep refilling it.

a He even worked as a hypnotist for a short time.
b He made a thick ink like a paste.
c He sold his first pens to the British and American governments.
d Lewis Waterman invented the fountain pen in 1884.
e Many companies now make ballpoint pens, but most people in the English-speaking world call all ballpoint pens *biros*.
f The ballpoint pen was not a new idea – John Loud invented it in 1888.
g They wanted to escape the advance of Hitler.

Lesson 4: Applying new skills

You are going to write about another important invention in the field of communications.

Ⓐ Imagine you have written the summary. It contains all the topic sentences.

Complete each sentence with a suitable verb in the correct form.

1 Guglielmo Marconi _____ in 1874 in Italy.

2 As a teenager, he started _____ experiments with electrical signals.

3 It was already possible _____ electrical signals with wires.

4 Marconi was not the first person _____ about sending electrical signals without wires.

5 By 1894, Marconi _____ to send signals across his laboratory.

6 Marconi _____ the Italian government for help with developing his invention, but they _____.

7 In 1897, he _____ the Marconi Wireless Telegraph and Signal Company.

8 Marconi _____ his first radios to the owners of ships.

9 On 12th December, 1901, Marconi _____ a signal from the UK to the USA.

10 When Marconi _____ in 1937, there _____ 100 million regular listeners to radio programmes.

Ⓑ Read each topic sentence in Exercise A. What extra information will a reader expect to find in each paragraph?

Ⓒ You have made a list of extra information for your text. Which paragraph (1–10) are you going to put each piece of extra information in?

P	Contents
	early successes
	Marconi's company
	parents and early life
	radio signals between UK and USA
	radios on ships
	the spread of radio
	other inventions in the same field
	other inventors in the same field
	problems with the invention
	reasons for interest in electrical signals

1900 = 2 ships collided off USA; radio signal brought help; 1,650 people saved; M = famous.

James Maxwell (1860) = 'possible';
Heinrich Hertz = produced radio waves (1880s)

M = move to England;
Br. gov. interested then not interested!
M = 'develop invention myself'

M's Br. relatives = 'We'll help with cost'; 1897 = sent signal >14 km.

mother = English; father = Italian
M = 16 = laboratory in family home

M realised = send signals further with high aerials;
M's brother took receiver away from house = still picked up the signal

Samuel Morse invented telegraph years before;
1,000s km. of telegraph wire across US when M = born

today = 1,000s radio stations; 2.5 billion radios

UK – USA = c5,000 km;
scientists = 'impossible! signals will go straight into space'
but signals bounced
off atmosphere

M wanted to send signals without wires

Ⓓ You have discussed the pieces of information in the yellow box. Which paragraph should each piece go in, i.e., which topic sentence should it follow?

Ⓔ Write the complete essay.

1 Copy the topic sentences from Exercise A.

2 Find the correct set of notes in Exercise D to continue the paragraph.

3 Expand the notes into full sentences.

Example:

Guglielmo Marconi was born in 1874 in Italy. His mother was English, but his father was Italian. When he was only 16, he set up a laboratory in the family home.

In this theme you are going to tell a story from world literature.

Lesson 1: Vocabulary

You are going to learn some vocabulary to help you write the text.

A Discuss these questions. They use some of the red words.

1 What kind of a play is *Hamlet*?
2 Who is the writer of the play?
3 Who are the main characters in the play?
4 Who does Hamlet kill?
5 What is the plot of the play, in one sentence?

B Read the text. Write a red or green word in each space. Make any necessary changes. Use a dictionary to check your ideas.

Shakespeare did not invent the _____ of most of his plays. He used the stories and plays of other _____. For his Histories, he also used historical _____. For his _____, like *Hamlet, Prince of Denmark*, he used ancient stories.

   The original _____ of the *Hamlet* story is a book in Latin by Saxo Grammaticus called *Historia Danica*, or *The History of the Danes*. This book appeared around 1200. The main _____ in this story is called Amlethus.

   A French _____ of the Saxo story appeared in 1576. It is possible that Shakespeare read this _____, but there was also an old play in English with the same _____. There are no copies of the play today, but people think that it was very similar. It had the same _____ of *Hamlet*. It had the same _____ of Denmark. People think that it had the same _____ of a mother who marries her husband's murderer. They also think that it had the same _____, with everybody dead. It certainly had the same _____ of revenge. Hamlet wants revenge on his uncle for his father's death.

C The text tells us that Shakespeare took his titles, settings, plots, endings and themes from other writers. How do you feel about this?

character *(n)*

kill *(v)*

play *(n)*

plot *(n)*

tragedy *(n)*

writer *(n)*

ending *(n)*

setting *(n)*

source *(n)*

theme *(n)*

title *(n)*

translation *(n)*

Lesson 2: Writing

You are going to write about a famous play by Shakespeare.

A Look at the research notes in Table 1 opposite. Which question does each section answer? Write the heading in the space.

1 Who are the main characters? <u>Characters</u>
2 When did he write it? _____
3 How does it end? _____
4 Where does it take place? _____
5 Where did he get the story from? _____

6 What happens? _____
7 What is it about? _____
8 When does it take place? _____
9 What is it called? _____
10 What kind of play is it? _____

B Organise the headings into paragraphs.

1 How many paragraphs do you need?
2 What heading can you give to each paragraph?
3 What will be the main tense in each paragraph? Explain your choices.

C Write your paragraphs.

Lesson 3: Learning new skills

A There is one word missing from each of these sentences. What is the word? Where does it go? Rewrite each sentence in your exercise book.

1 William Shakespeare wrote *Othello* 1601 and 1604.
2 It is tragedy.
3 The play takes place Venice and Cyprus.
4 The time is late 16th century.
5 Shakespeare probably got the story from a play by Cinthio, *The Moor of Venice*.
6 However, there no English translation at the time of Shakespeare.
7 Is possible that Shakespeare read a French version from 1584.
8 The play is about Othello, a Venetian general, and wife Desdemona.
9 Othello kills his wife and then that she is innocent.
10 Everyone says Iago is honest he is dishonest.

B You are going to tell the story of the plot in more detail.

1 Read Skills Check 1.
2 Complete the story of the plot opposite. Use a verb from the box in each space. Put it in the correct form.

C The plot opposite does not contain any pronouns or possessive adjectives.

1 Read Skills Check 2.
2 Find good places for pronouns and possessive adjectives.
3 Rewrite the plot with pronouns, different nouns and possessive adjectives.

D Exchange plots with a partner. Can you understand who each word refers to?

Skills Check 1

Writing a plot

In English we usually write the plot of a play, novel or film in the present simple.
Example: *Othello kills his wife.*

Skills Check 2

Using pronouns

You know about using pronouns the second, third, etc., time that a person or thing appears. However, we must use a noun if there is any chance of the reader being confused.
Example: *Iago is a soldier. **He** expects to become Othello's lieutenant, but Othello promotes another man instead. **Iago** is angry with Othello …*

Table 1: Research notes on Shakespeare play

Title	Othello
Date	*Between 1601 and 1604*
Setting	*In Venice and Cyprus*
Time	*In the late 16th C, during the wars between Venice and Turkey*
Type	*Tragedy*
Characters	*Othello, a Venetian general; Desdemona, his wife; Iago, a Venetian soldier*
Plot	*I. tells O. 'D. = loves another man'*
Ending	*O. kills D. then finds out D = innocent*
Sources	*Perhaps **The Moor of Venice** by Cinthio (1565) = short play = all the main characters and events of Sh. play.* *BUT* *no Eng. trans. at time of Sh.* *Did Sh. read Fr. version (1584)?*
Themes	*1. What is truth?* *Everyone says I. = honest but = dishonest* *O. thinks D. guilty but = innocent* *2. Pride* *O. = proud of himself, achievements, new wife* *O. = 'D. loves another man' so = v. angry* *3. Good versus evil:* *D. = good I. = evil* *Sh. says 'Good person ➔ evil person'* *Who wins? Don't know because everybody = dead*

The plot

be bring commit condemn decide expect find follow get go kill love make murder promote run tell try

Othello _____ a general in the Venetian army. Desdemona _____ the daughter of a Venetian senator. Othello and Desdemona _____ married. Othello and Desdemona _____ to build a life together. It is not easy for Othello and Desdemona because there _____ big differences in Othello's and Desdemona's ages and experience of the world.

Iago _____ a soldier in the Venetian army. Iago _____ to become Othello's lieutenant, but Othello _____ a man called Cassio instead. Iago _____ angry with Othello and _____ to destroy Othello's marriage. Iago _____ Othello believe that Desdemona _____ Cassio. Othello _____ Desdemona. Emilia _____ Iago's wife and Desdemona's servant. Emilia _____ Desdemona's body and _____ Iago about Othello's crime. Then Iago _____ Emilia about Iago's actions. Emilia _____ and tells Othello. Iago _____ Emilia then _____ away, but soldiers _____ Iago and _____ Iago back. Othello _____ Iago to death then _____ suicide.

Lesson 4: Applying new skills

A Imagine you write the paragraphs below about *Othello*. Then you find extra pieces of information (right).

1 Choose the best paragraph for each piece of information.
2 Decide the best place in the paragraph for the information.
3 Rewrite the paragraphs, including the extra information.

It is possible that Shakespeare read a French translation of the Cinthio play from 1584.

Othello is proud of his achievements.

Othello is a tragedy.

Othello thinks Desdemona is guilty, whereas in fact she is innocent.

Shakespeare says in the play that a good person can become evil.

At the end of the play, everybody dies.

Iago is angry with Othello because he doesn't promote him.

Background

William Shakespeare wrote *Othello* between 1601 and 1604. The play takes place in Venice and Cyprus. The time is the late 16th century, during the wars between Venice and Turkey.

Sources

Shakespeare probably got the story from a play by Cinthio called *The Moor of Venice*. It appeared in 1565. However, there was no English translation at the time of Shakespeare.

The plot

The play is about Othello, a Venetian general, his wife Desdemona, and a Venetian soldier called Iago. Iago tells Othello that his wife loves a man called Cassio. Othello kills his wife and then finds out that she is innocent.

The themes

There are three main themes in Othello:
The first theme is 'What is truth?' Everyone calls Iago honest, whereas in fact he is dishonest. The second theme is pride. Othello is proud of himself and his new wife. Perhaps this is why he gets so angry and kills her. The third theme is good versus evil. Desdemona represents good, whereas Iago represents evil. At the end, it is not clear whether good or evil wins, because everybody is dead.

B You are going to write about a piece of literature from your culture.

1 Copy Table 1.
2 Do some research to complete the table with notes.
3 Organise the information into four paragraphs:
   • Background
   • Sources
   • The plot
   • The themes

C Write a first draft.

D Exchange drafts with your partner. Compare the draft and the notes. Talk to your partner about problems with spelling or grammar.

Table 1: Research notes

Writer	
Title	
Date	
Setting	
Time	
Type	
Sources	
Characters	
Plot	
Themes	

In this theme you are going to write about the Olympic Games.

Lesson I: Vocabulary

You are going to learn some vocabulary that you will need to write about the Games.

A Look at the red words for 30 seconds. Then cover the words and add the vowels.

1 ch___ ___se   4 pl__y__r
2 eq___ __pm__nt   5 r__l__
3 g__m__   6 t__ __m

B Choose a sport. Then answer these questions, which use the red words.

1 What equipment do you need to play the game?
2 How many players are there in each team?
3 What are some of the rules?
4 What do the players try to do in the game?

C In Lesson 2 you are going to read about a sport at the Olympic Games. Here is an introduction to the text. Choose a green word or phrase for each space. Make any necessary changes.

The decathlon is probably the hardest _____ at the Olympic Games. It involves ten different sports. _____ in the decathlon must run fast, jump high and long, and throw things a long way. The athletes don't really _____ against each other. They get _____ for their results in each event. For example, a world _____ time for the 100 metres _____ over 1,000 points. Who _____? The athlete with the highest number of points at the end of the 10 sports. You don't have to win every sport, but the _____ of the event is usually the best in most of them. However, in 2000 Erki Nool didn't win a single sport but he won the _____ .

choose *(v)*

equipment *(n)*

game *(n)*

player *(n)*

rule *(n)*

team *(n)*

try *(v)*

athlete *(n)*

compete *(v)*

event *(n)*

gold medal *(n)*

point *(n)*

record *(n)*

score *(v)*

win *(v)*

winner *(n)*

D Study the green words. Which words ...

1 have a doubled letter?
2 end in *e*?
3 have three consonants together?
4 have two vowels together?
5 have the same vowel twice (but not together)?

Lesson 2: Writing

Skills Check 1

(A) Read the topic sentences below. Together they make a summary of a text about an Olympic event. Complete the text with the correct form of a suitable verb in each space.

Revision

Remember: Topic sentences should make a summary of a text (Theme 7). Write the topic sentences first, then write the rest of each paragraph.

1 The decathlon _____ its name from an ancient Greek word meaning 'ten athletic sports'.
2 The modern Olympic Games _____ in 1896 in Athens, Greece.
3 The decathlon _____ not an event at the first modern Olympics.
4 A native American, Jim Thorpe, _____ the first Olympic decathlon.
5 The king of Sweden _____ Thorpe his gold medal.
6 The current Olympic champion _____ Erki Nool of Estonia.
7 The final scores in 2000 _____ very close.
8 Erki Nool's winning score in 2000 _____ very high.

(B) What sort of information do you expect to find in the other sentences of each paragraph above?
1 Match each topic sentence to a paragraph from the text opposite.
2 Write the correct topic sentence for each paragraph. Number the paragraphs in order.

(C) Read the whole text – topic sentences and the rest of each paragraph – in order. Complete the research notes under the text.

(D) Cover the text. Write five sentences from the information in your research notes.

Lesson 3: Learning new skills

(A) Write three sentences using some of the words from the yellow box.

athlete beat champion place win event
score victory title record

(B) How can you compare more than two things in English? There is a mistake in each of these sentences.
1 Find the mistake.
2 Read Skills Check 2 and check your answers.
3 Check with the text opposite.
   a The king said to Thorpe, 'You are the greater athlete in the world.'
   b However, Nool's victory was not closest in history.
   c The winning margin of 999 points is the bigest in Olympic history.
   d However, it was not the highest in the history.
   e He was 35, the olddest decathlon medal winner in history.

Skills Check 2

Comparing more than two things

We use **superlative adjectives** to compare more than two things.
Examples:
The winning margin is **the biggest** in history.
You are **the greatest** athlete in the world.
We make the superlative with *the* + adj + *est*, but if the adj ends in:
1 e = add st, e.g., *largest*
2 CVC = double C = e.g., *biggest*
3 y = change to i, e.g., *heaviest*

(C) Find and underline 10 pronouns in the text on the opposite page. Work out what each pronoun refers to.

	He defeated the local hero, Charles Lomberg of Sweden. He scored 8,412 points, while Lomberg got 7,413. The winning margin of 999 points is still the biggest in Olympic history.
	He won the title 'the greatest athlete' at the 2000 Olympics in Sydney, Australia. His score was 8,641 points. Roman Sebrle of the Czech Republic was in second place, with 8,606 points. Third place went to Chris Huffins of the USA. He was 35, the oldest decathlon medal winner in history.
	However, it is not the highest in history. The Olympic record holder is Dan O'Brien of the USA. He scored 8,824 points at the 1996 Games in Atlanta, USA.
	However, Nool's victory was not the closest in history. In 1920, Helge Lovland of Norway beat Brutus Hamilton of the USA by only 33 points.
	It appeared at the 1912 Games in Stockholm, Sweden. The event consists of ten athletic sports involving running, jumping and throwing.
The decathlon takes its name from a word in ancient Greek meaning 'ten athletic sports'.	It is quite a modern event. However, it grew out of the pentathlon ('five athletic sports') in the ancient Olympic Games. The pentathlon consisted of jumping, throwing, running and wrestling events.
	The king said to Thorpe, 'You are the greatest athlete in the world.' The title stuck! The decathlon champion at each Olympics is still called 'the greatest athlete in the world' for four years, at least.
	They were the idea of Baron de Coubertin from France. Coubertin believed that physical education was very important. He also thought that international sport helped to prevent international war.

Sport	*Decathlon*
First appearance at Games	
History	
First champion	
Winning points / time, etc.	
Second place	
Current champion	
Winning points / time, etc.	
Second place	
Olympic record holder	
Olympic record	
Record set at	

Lesson 4: Applying new skills

Ⓐ We have seen before that information appears in an English sentence in several common patterns.

1 Find three pairs of sentences below with the same pattern.

2 Explain the pattern.

3 Write one new sentence with each pattern. You can invent the information.

    a He beat Charles Lomberg of Sweden in 1912.

    b He scored 8,824 points at the 1996 Games in Atlanta, USA.

    c The modern Olympic Games started in 1896 in Athens, Greece.

    d He defeated Brutus Hamilton of the USA in 1920.

    e He won the title at the 2000 Olympics in Sydney in Australia.

    f The decathlon appeared at the 1912 Games in Stockholm in Sweden.

Ⓑ Read the Skills Check. Then write a new sentence in each case to give the same information in a different way. Begin with the words given.

1 The current Olympic Champion is Erki Nool.
   The Olympic champion ...

2 Jim Thorpe beat Charles Lomberg.
   Jim Thorpe came ...

3 He scored 8,641 points.
   His ...

4 Roman Sebrle came second.
   Roman Sebrle was in ...

5 Dan O'Brien is the current record holder.
   The current ...

Ⓒ You are going to write about another Olympic sport.

1 Choose a sport that you are interested in.

2 Do some research to complete Table I.

3 Write a summary of the information in six or eight topic sentences.

4 Write the rest of each paragraph. Write similar pieces of information in different ways.

Ⓓ Exchange drafts with a partner. Check the information with your partner's research notes. Mark spelling, punctuation and grammar mistakes.

Ⓔ Correct any mistakes and make a second draft. Give the second draft to your teacher.

> ### Skills Check
>
> #### Write it a different way
>
> It is often useful to be able to write information in different ways.
>
> **Example:**
>
> *The current Olympic champion is Erki Nool.*
> OR
> *The Olympic champion at the moment is Erki Nool.*
> OR
> *Erki Nool is the current champion.*

Table 1: Research notes on an Olympic sport

Sport	
First appearance at Games	
History	
First champion	
Winning points / time, etc.	
Second place	
Current champion	
Winning points / time, etc.	
Second place	
Olympic record holder	
Olympic record	
Record set at	

In this theme you are going to write about nutrition and studying.

Lesson 1: Vocabulary

You are going to learn some vocabulary that you will need to write about nutrition and studying.

Ⓐ Look at the red words for one minute.
   1 Cover the words and try to remember a word with:
     a *ch.*   **e** *ea.*
     b double *n.*   **f** *ie.*
     c double *o.*   **g** *a* twice – but not together.
     d *ou.*   **h** *o* twice – but not together.
   2 Uncover the red words. Check your answers.

Ⓑ Find pairs of red words. Explain the connection.
   Example: dinner – lunch = *two meals*

Ⓒ Write a green word or phrase next to each definition. Check with your dictionary.

	1 sweets, crisps, etc., with low nutritional value; **2** fast food like burgers, fried chicken
	main nutrient in foods like potatoes, bread, rice
	1 natural substance in animals; **2** part of meat, usually on the outside
	main nutrient in eggs, fish, etc.
	unit of measurement for energy value of food
	1 all the food that you eat; **2** special set of foods, usually to help you to lose weight

Ⓓ Write one of the green words or phrases in each space.

The normal _____ of people in the Western World is very different now from 50 years ago. In those days, people got most of their _____ from _____ in bread and potatoes. They got _____ from eggs and fish. Many people nowadays get most of their carbohydrate and protein from _____. This food has a lot of _____ , but it also has a lot of _____ .

Ⓔ This is your next assignment.
   1 Read the assignment.
   2 Do you believe that some foods or drinks help you to concentrate or improve your marks? If you do, which ones? If you don't, why not?
   3 How can you do research for this assignment …
     a in the library?
     b on the Internet?
   4 What sections should you have in your report?

bowl (*n*)

cook (*v*)

dinner (*n*)

fried (*adj*)

lunch (*n*)

potato/es (*n*)

salad (*n*)

soup (*n*)

steak (*n*)

breakfast cereal (*n*)

calorie/s (*n*)

carbohydrate (*n*)

diet (*n*)

fat (*n*)

junk food (*n*)

protein (*n*)

Greenhill College   Food Science Faculty

ASSIGNMENT 3: Nutrition and Studying

Consider these questions:
- Is there any connection between food and drinks and studying?
- Do some foods or drinks help you to concentrate or improve your marks?

Do some research in the library or on the Internet.
Write a report.
Be careful! Some sources are reliable, some are not.

Lesson 2: Writing review (1)

A You will need many different sentence patterns for your assignment. In this course you have studied the patterns below. There is one mistake in each pattern – extra word, missing word, wrong word or wrong word order. Find the mistakes and correct them.

1 Both Kuwait or Qatar are small countries.
2 I not believe that parents should make fun of idealism.
3 If teenagers admire bad role models, they may to copy their behaviour.
4 The UK is in Western Europe, where the USA is part of the North American continent.
5 I think that parents follow their own advice.
6 The women sing during the ceremony songs.
7 There are too many similarities between Muslim weddings in India and in Arabia.
8 There also are some differences.
9 Washington, DC, is hotter in summer then London.
10 We considered several ways of spend the money.
11 The Olympic decathlete is greatest athlete in the world.
12 In the future I work harder.

B Complete these sentences. They are all about nutrition and health. They use some of the patterns from Exercise A.

1 Both coffee and …
2 I don't believe that people …
3 If people eat junk food, …
4 Salads are good for you, whereas …
5 I think that college canteens …
6 There are many similarities …
7 … best food in the world.
8 Water is better …

C Choose four of the patterns in Exercise C above. Write one more sentence about nutrition and health.

D Scan the research information on the opposite page.
1 Where do you think each piece of information comes from?
2 Why is this important?
3 What are you looking for in this information?

E Read the information in numbers 1 to 7 opposite. Make notes in the table below under Source 1. What does it say about these foods and drinks?

F Read the information in numbers 8 to 14 opposite. Make notes in the table below under Source 2.

G Which sources do you think are more reliable? Why?

Food / Drink	Source 1	Source 2
fish		
green vegetables		
breakfast		
junk food		
coffee		
water		
soft drinks		

1 # Did you know ...

fish is good for the brain?
It helps you to concentrate.

tuna
mackerel } = omega 3 = makes brain cells
cod   (fatty acid)   work properly

8
Fish = good for the brain ✓✓✓
BUT
Omega 3 = helps brain cells of babies to
develop (inc. unborn babies)
No effect on adults!!!

2 ## Eat your greens!

Green vegetables have lots of good things in them. Cabbage and broccoli, for example, are full of iron — and if you don't have enough iron, you will feel tired and lazy. Eat your greens just before an important exam — and go to the top of the class!

9
Green vegetables = v. good for you
BUT
must be part of a healthy diet
= not help pass an exam / do better
assignment

3 IT IS NOW CLEAR to everybody that breakfast is the most important meal of the day. Get off to a great start with a full English breakfast – fried eggs, sausages, tomatoes, mushrooms. It's the best way to start your day.

10
Fried food is full of fat. The human body uses a lot of energy to break down fat. That's why you feel tired for several hours after a big cooked meal.

4 High-carbohydrate, low-sugar foods are the best things to eat for breakfast because:
1. They help you to concentrate.
2. They stop you feeling hungry.

11
Breakfast cereals, bread =
high in carbohydrate, low in sugar

5 ### Junk food helps with maths and English

Researchers at the University of Florida report that junk food for lunch can help students in maths and English tests. "Junk food, like burgers and French fries, contains high calories," said one of the researchers. "These calories increase the supply of energy to the brain."

12 ## Junk food makes you sleepy

Scientists say that junk foods like fried chicken do not help with concentration or exam success. "Junk food is high in protein and fat. These foods make you feel tired," the head of one research lab told our reporter.

6 ### Wake up to
Quickcafe ☀

The instant way to start the day.

Feeling tired?
Busy day ahead?
Working?
Studying?
Taking exams?

A quick cup of Quickcafe and you're wide awake.

7 ### Why do we need water?
– to wash ⇒ toxins out of your blood
– for all the cells of your body
How much water do we need?
– eight to 12 glasses a day (American Dietetic Association)
Can I have a soft drink instead of water?
Most soft drinks contain a lot of sugar. The sugar slows down the process, so the water takes longer to get into the blood.

13 **Caffeine** – a substance in coffee, tea, many soft drinks and bars of chocolate, etc. Caffeine acts as a stimulant and makes you feel more awake; after having a drink with caffeine you should drink lots of water to reduce the side-effects (see Table 1).

Table 1 Amount of caffeine (in mg)

cup of coffee	135
cup of tea	50
glass of cola	35
coffee ice-cream	50
coffee yoghurt	45
chocolate bar	30

14 **Toxin** – a poison in the body. The body makes toxins after eating some types of food, e.g., junk food. If you don't wash the toxins out, you will feel tired.

Lesson 3: Writing review (2)

(A) The words on the right make phrases and expressions from the research information (Lesson 2).
1 Match the words and write each phrase.
2 Decide if you need a hyphen (-) between the words.
3 Make a good sentence with five of the expressions.

a	brain	1	acid
b	breakfast	2	carbohydrate
c	fatty	3	cells
d	green	4	cereal
e	healthy	5	diet
f	high	6	effect
g	important	7	food
h	junk	8	meal
i	low	9	sugar
j	side	10	vegetables

(B) In this course you have learnt to write topic sentences. Complete these topic sentences with a suitable verb in each space.

Topic sentences	Notes for the rest of the paragraph
1 Some people _____ that fish _____ good for the brain.	
2 Some scientists _____ that green vegetables _____ useful.	
3 Most researchers _____ that students should _____ the day with a good breakfast.	
4 I _____ several pieces of research about junk food.	
5 I also _____ some extra ideas about coffee and other products.	
6 All researchers _____ drinking lots of water.	

(C) In this course you have learnt that topic sentences should make a summary of the text. The topic sentences in Exercise D make a good summary of the assignment. What extra information are you going to put in each paragraph?

(D) In this course you have learnt to compare two things. Look back at the table of notes at the end of Lesson 2. Write one sentence each, comparing the information in each source.
Example: *Some people say that fish like tuna helps you to concentrate, while other people say the fatty acids only help the brain cells of babies to develop.*

Lesson 4: Writing review (3)

(A) Write the **Findings** of your assignment. Use the topic sentences from Lesson 3 Exercise C. Write the rest of the paragraph using your notes from Exercise D.

(B) Write the **Introduction** to your assignment. Answer these questions:
1 What is this reprt about?
2 How do you do your research?

(C) Write the **Conclusion** to your assignment. It must be logical from the information in the **Findings** section.

(D) Follow the usual procedure with the first draft and second draft.

THEME 1
Education, How Do You Revise?

assignment *(n)*

diploma *(n)*

draft *(n)*

faculty *(n)*

form *(n)*

instructor *(n)*

literature *(n)*

doubled *(adj)*

link *(v)*

multiple *(adj)*

open *(adj)*

organise *(v)*

practice *(n)*

relevant *(adj)*

revise *(v)*

silent *(adj)*

THEME 2
Daily Life, Parents and Teenagers

always *(adv)*

never *(adv)*

often *(adj)*

once *(adj)*

schedule *(n)*

social *(adj)*

sometimes *(adv)*

twice *(adv)*

usually *(adv)*

weekly *(adv)*

adult *(n)*

decision *(n)*

parent *(n)*

teenager *(n)*

THEME 3
Work and Business, How to Spend $10,000

applicant *(n)*

assist *(v)*

benefit *(n)*

employment *(n)*

overtime *(n)*

salary *(n)*

administrator *(n)*

conclude *(v)*

equipment *(n)*

furniture *(n)*

purchase *(v)*

recommendation *(n)*

report *(n)*

resource *(n)*

THEME 4
Science and Nature, The 8th Wonder of the World?

average *(adj)*

decrease *(n)*

graph *(n)*

increase *(n)*

steady *(adj)*

unit of measurement *(n)*

achieve *(v)*

aim *(n)*

construct *(v)*

facts and figures *(n)*

fresh (water) *(adj)*

project *(n)*

structure *(n)*

THEME 5
The Physical World,
The UK and the USA

continent (n)

fertile (adj)

region (n)

the Equator (n)

agriculture (n)

area (n)

border (n)

climate (n)

continent (n)

industry (n)

location (n)

main (adj)

population (n)

THEME 6
Culture and Civilization,
There Are Two
Ceremonies

balloon (n)

festival (n)

harvest (n)

neighbour (n)

parade (n)

bride (n)

ceremony(ies) (n)

engagement (n)

groom (n)

marriage (n)

married (adj)

wedding (n)

THEME 7
They Made Our World,
Biro and Marconi

control (v)

drove (v)

flew (v)

invent (v)

jet (n)

navy (n)

rode (v)

row (v)

sailed (v)

submarine (n)

decide (v)

develop (v)

produce (v)

reach (v)

realise (v)

sell (v)

solve (v)

think of (v)

work (v) (= do the
job correctly)

THEME 8
Art and Literature,
Othello

character (n)

kill (v)

play (n)

plot (n)

tragedy (n)

writer (n)

ending (n)

setting (n)

source (n)

theme (n)

title (n)

translation (n)

THEME 9
Sports and Leisure, The Greatest Athlete in the World

choose *(v)*

equipment *(n)*

game *(n)*

player *(n)*

rule *(n)*

team *(n)*

try *(v)*

athlete *(n)*

compete *(v)*

event *(n)*

gold medal *(n)*

point *(n)*

record *(n)*

score *(v)*

win *(v)*

winner *(n)*

THEME 10
Nutrition and Health, Fish Is Good for Your Brain

bowl *(n)*

cook *(v)*

dinner *(n)*

fried *(adj)*

lunch *(n)*

potato/es *(n)*

salad *(n)*

soup *(n)*

steak *(n)*

breakfast cereal *(n)*

calorie/s *(n)*

carbohydrate *(n)*

diet *(n)*

fat *(n)*

junk food *(n)*

protein *(n)*

---

achieve *(v)*

administrator *(n)*

adult *(n)*

agriculture *(n)*

aim *(n)*

always *(adv)*

applicant *(n)*

area *(n)*

assignment *(n)*

assist *(v)*

athlete *(n)*

average *(adj)*

balloon *(n)*

benefit *(n)*

border *(n)*

bowl *(n)*

breakfast cereal *(n)*

bride *(n)*

calorie/s *(n)*

carbohydrate *(n)*

ceremony(ies) *(n)*

character *(n)*

choose *(v)*

climate *(n)*

compete *(v)*

---

conclude *(v)*

construct *(v)*

continent *(n)*

continent *(n)*

control *(n)*

cook *(v)*

decide *(v)*

decision *(n)*

decrease *(n)*

develop *(v)*

diet *(n)*

dinner *(n)*

diploma *(n)*

doubled *(adj)*

draft *(n)*

drove *(v)*

employment *(n)*

ending *(n)*

engagement *(n)*

equipment *(n)*

equipment *(n)*

event *(n)*

facts and figures *(n)*

faculty *(n)*

fat *(n)*

fertile (adj)

festival (n)

flew (v)

form (n)

fresh (water) (adj)

fried (adj)

furniture (n)

game (n)

gold medal (n)

graph (n)

groom (n)

harvest (n)

industry (n)

instructor (n)

invent (v)

jet (n)

junk food (n)

kill (v)

link (v)

literature (n)

location (n)

lunch (n)

main (adj)

marriage (n)

married (adj)

multiple (adj)

navy (n)

neighbour (n)

never (adv)

often (adj)

once (adj)

open (adj)

organise (v)

overtime (n)

parade (n)

parent (n)

phase (n)

play (n)

player (n)

plot (n)

point (n)

population (n)

potato/es (n)

practice (n)

produce (v)

progress report (n)

project (n)

protein (n)

purchase (v)

reach (v)

realise (v)

recommendation (n)

record (n)

region (n)

relevant (adj)

report (n)

resource (n)

revise (v)

rode (v)

row (v)

rule (n)

sailed (v)

salad (n)

salary (n)

schedule (n)

score (v)

sell (v)

setting (n)

silent (adj)

social (adv)

solve (v)

sometimes (adv)

soup (n)

source (n)

steady (adj)

steak (n)

structure (n)

submarine (n)

team (n)

teenager (n)

the Equator (n)

theme (n)

think of (v)

title (n)

tragedy (n)

translation (n)

try (v)

twice (adv)

unit of
measurement (n)

usually (adv)

wedding (n)

weekly (adv)

win (v)

winner (n)

work (v) (= do the
job correctly)

writer (n)